after her.

by january black.

IIJIMA
press

After Her.

January Black.

— to the women
who walk this world,

for the men
who've let them
walk out of theirs.

"...and, you'll always love me, won't you?"

"...yes."

"...and the rain won't make any difference?"

"...no."

— **ernest hemingway**, *a farewell to arms*

"my love gun's loaded

and she's in my sights

big game is waiting there

inside her tights."

— **spinal tap**, *big bottom*

who the fuck is january black?

i suppose this is a splendid time
for me to introduce myself.
there is a very good chance
you don't know who the fuck i am.
my name is january.
january black.
i'm the alter ego of some sonofabitch
named cole schafer.
you've probably never heard of him.
he's almost famous
in the world of advertising.
less so in the world of prose.
he and i are very alike in many ways.
we're not alike at all in others.
i'm better looking than cole.
i've got a fuller head of hair than cole.
i've got more tattoos than cole.
i've done a hell of a lot better with women than cole.
i'm a better writer than cole.
i have a bigger dick than cole.
truth be told, i am cole.
i'm just everything cole wishes he could be.
i'm all the ugly parts about himself he's too afraid to reveal.
but unlike cole, i have schizophrenia.
well, cole has it too.
but, only when he's on the page
with a pen in his hand.

i on the other hand,
was diagnosed after her.
i was twenty-six.
the year was twenty-twenty.
it was the year the world went to shit.
░░░░░░░░░░ting gunned down in the streets
an░ ░░░░ ░░░ picked up something nasty
from a snake
or a buzzard
or who the fuck knows what
at an outdoor market
that killed millions of people worldwide.
that year,
a cough became a guillotine.
it was right around here
when i started seeing shit.
i went to my doctor and i said,

"doctor,
i think i'm seeing things
that aren't there."

and, he said,

"elaborate".

and, i said,

"doctor, there's a nurse
that looks like marilyn monroe

to the right of you,
she's licking her fingers
and touching herself."

he stared at me
with what jane austen calls
a quizzical brow,
and i know it took
every ounce of his sanity
not to turn around.

finally,
he smiled.
he winked at me.
he said,

"it doesn't sound
like a bad problem to have.
though,
we should get you checked out"

he wrote a name down
on a piece of paper
with a big black pen
that bled through like a newspaper
left to the elements
and i visited that name
on that piece of paper
where i was prescribed these pills
that were meant to help me

not see the things everyone else couldn't see.

so i'm not sure if any of this is real
or if all of it is real.

but
it's pretty.

it's awfully
fucking pretty.

before her.

five.

his hands are still there,
two decades later,
all over me,
reminding me
it's all make-up
— the racks
and the tattoos
and the lovely words
and the pretty faces
— it's all make-up
covering up
that little boy
locked in the bathroom.

vulnerable.

sometimes
i
feel
like
i'm
looking
at
the
world
behind
a
two
way
mirror.

five (again).

i'm five.
something bad happens.
i don't know it
at the time.

i don't know it
because growing up
you're told to listen to adults.

it happens several times
in a bathroom with ugly wallpaper.

we move houses.

my new room in the new house
has a new bathroom in it.

my momma asks me
why i always shut the bathroom door.

i tell her i prefer it that way.

i don't say:

there are monsters in there.

dark nights in southern indiana.

my
momma said

if i get lost
catching fireflies,

i should use them
to light my way

back home.

southern indiana baby, baby.

i was born and raised in
southern indiana:

falling
for the feeling of bare feet,
stampeding,
on cold grass,

chasing
the twinkle of fireflies,
piercing,
the black canvas of a summer night sky,

macking
on pretty girls,
dancing,
in crammed river camps
by moonlit waters,

smelling
bug repellant,
perfuming,
mosquito kissed skin,

falling
in love,
over and over again,

in that small town of newburgh
nestled by the ohio.

two doors down.

growing up,
she and i lived
in the same neighborhood.
we'd ride the school bus home together
and sometimes
i'd go over to her house
and we'd play
the way kids play.
i've been there
at strange moments in her life.
she always had the thickest hair
and once
when she was four or five or six,
she took a pair of fiskars
and cut heaps of it off.
it fucked her momma up good
when she saw her sheared locks
spread across the carpet
like fallen tassels.
i think it kind of fucked me up,
too.
i still hate it
when pretty girls cut their hair.
we're all grown up now
and in faraway places
and on rare occasions
we'll find ourselves in the same city

and when we do,
we're like magnets.
it's always been this way.
she's not my human.
but she feels something close to it on nights
when she's drunk
and i'm drunk
and by happenstance,
we end up at the same club or bar or haunt.
we play it cool, at first.
but, sooner or later
we'll strike up a conversation
we shouldn't be having
and we'll start looking at each other
in ways we shouldn't be looking
and before we find ourselves doing something
we shouldn't be doing,
one of our homies
will pull us away.
and,
i'll ride home
in an uber or a cab,
alone,
smoking a cigarette
until the driver tells me to put it out,
wondering whether our childhood crushes
ever truly fade away.

fuck them so good they say 'jesus'.

those pretty
christian girls
will break your heart,

boy.

you're good-lookin'
but you
can't
compete
with god,

boy.

puberty.

my english teacher in middle school
had bleach blonde hair
and enormous breasts.

she was a tragedy
for a boy in puberty.

i spent most of the class
with an erection.
she'd call me up
to the front of the room
to write a sentence on the board.

i'd stand up,
slowly
tuck my dick
in my waistband
and do a sort of awkward crab shuffle
up the claustrophobic aisles
between the desks,
praying,
the sonofabitch wouldn't
slip out and graze
one of my classmate's ears.

eldest.

i'm scared of growing old
with someone
and running out
of things to talk about.

or,
forgetting the things
we talk about.

urgency.

some
of
us
are
living
as
if
there
is
no
such
thing
as
getting
hit
by
a

bus.

just north of hell.

it's a few decades from now.
i'm sitting pretty
in an underground pub
in the basement of a flower shop.
god is beside me,
his gold rings
adding additional decor
to the knuckle-worn bar top
battered with nicks and bruises,
artifacts of countless conversations
like the one we're having now.
i'm dead.
i'm not sure from what.
we're smoking cigarettes
and drinking moscow mules.
he likes me.
but,
says there's not a shot in hell
i'm getting in.
i laugh.
he laughs.
we talk bukowski
and hemingway
and woolf.

the lights begin to fade.

last call.

heaven, sin.

tell me,
do
angels
make
love?

and,
do
they
make
it
well?

fallen.

sometimes,
i feel like an angel
with big beating wings
flying between heaven and hell,
flirting with
heat-seeking missiles,
dodging them,
dodging them,
not dodging them,
clipping wings,
falling,
falling,
loving

the falling.

my fuck.

i'm not entirely sure what falling in love feels like
nor how to put the feeling
into words.

but,
if i were to try,
i would write:

it's not a feeling at all
but instead
a profound sense of responsibility
to another person.

it's a responsibility that fucks us up
because most of us go our entire lives
caring about no one else
but ourselves
and then one day,
out of nowhere,
we stumble upon this beautiful human being
and everything changes.

in this stumbling,
we become the truest
most beautiful
versions of ourselves
because for the first time in our lives

we care about someone more
than we care about ourselves.

i think that's what falling in love is.

it's staring your human in the eyes,
your eyes dilating
as your brain absorbs
every fabric of her smile
and thinking,

"my fuck,
maybe i was put on this earth
to care more about this human
than i care about myself."

brass check.

my dreams
are dragons.

i am killing off
those motherfuckers,
left and right.

i've got a trunk full
of their heads,
sitting in my closet,
and a bankroll full
of all the gold
they were guarding.

but no queen.

i'm certain how it goes.

he has big boisterous dreams
that keep him up at night,
that make his heart beat wildly,
that take him to faraway places.

he has these big boisterous dreams
that seem like the only thing
in the world that matters.

and the big boisterous dreams
never go away
but they grow quieter
as he falls in love
with the way her laughter
adds frequency to the room,
with the way that waterfall
she calls a head of hair
defies gravity when she ties it up
and into a bun,
with the way she hugs him
when he rolls over in his sleep
never wanting to let him go,
with the way her eyes
change colors in the sun,
with the way she goes silent
when she has everything to say
but can't seem to say anything at all,

with the way she feels like home.

i'm certain how it goes.

glancing, catching glances.

he's
looking
at
her
like
he
wants
to
for
the
rest
of
his
life.

past life.

— when i lock eyes
with

a good-looking stranger

i feel i've known
my whole life

i wonder

if the two of us
ran a kingdom
in a past life

and

i wonder

if we're up
for doing the
whole fucking thing again,

in this life.

natalie.

it's chicago,
forever ago.
i keep locking eyes
with this girl across the room.
she has a face out of a magazine
and dark skin festooned with
a lovely array of tattoos
that she wears like coco wore chanel.
i want to speak to her
but we are separated
by a sea of people,
illuminated,
by blaring lights.
lurking in this sea
are big carnivorous butterflies
she eventually fights them off,
walks up,
reaches out her hand
and introduces herself to me.

i don't let go.

bullfighter.

i'm locking eyes
(again)
with a girl sitting
window-side
at my favorite
chicago
coffee shop,
sipping tea,
she's got a ring
hanging
from her septum
like the mascot
jordan made famous
and she's staring at
me like
i am the matador.

i am the matador.

primal.

love-making is so primal.

it's our eyes dilating
to absorb more pretty.

it's wet dripping
to cushion the collision
of our bodies,
dancing.

it's foreheads pressing
skin-to-skin
so our brains can fuck,
too.

it's grabbing her neck,
both gently and less so,
to let her know
you're here,
that you've got hold
of the most vulnerable part of her
and you're not going to hurt her.

bpm.

i
press
my
lips
against
her
neck
and
feel
her
pulse
kiss
back.

distractions.

she's white but on this particular night
she looks like pocahontas.
her hair is painted black.
we're drinking wine
at a small winery
in southern indiana.
everyone is looking at her.
i'm looking at her.
she's looking famous.
we're getting a feel for one another.
i feel like i might be a distraction
from her missing someone,
which i'm okay with.
i'm in love with the idea
of helping her forget about missing
whomever it is
she is missing.
and i do.

wine with her
turns into
more wine at her place
and more wine at her place
turns into
me distracting her
without wine
and these distractions

lead to sleep
and in the morning
we switch out the wine
for coffee and it's exactly
as vonnegut writes —
everything is beautiful and nothing hurt.

we have a few more run-ins after this
and i imagine we will have a few more
because while we can't fall in love with distrac-
tions,
we certainly can learn to crave them.

pheel.

some
people
don't
like
to
feel
things.

these
aren't
the
people
for
me.

nyctophobia.

honey,
i'm
scared
of
the
dark.

so,

let
me
fuck
you
with
the
lights
on.

shower talk.

most young couples
do a lot of fucking
in the beginning.
they fuck on the floor
they fuck on the bed
they fuck in the shower
they fuck everywhere.
but,
eventually,
they have to talk to one another.
because as nice as fucking is,
you can't fuck everywhere.
you can't fuck at christmas dinner.
you can't fuck whilst driving
(at least not safely).
you can't fuck when her world is crashing down.
you can't fuck over coffee
(not without getting burnt).
instead,
you have to talk to one another.
and,
i've noticed it's talking
where things begin to go awry.
at least for me.

stretch marks.

i want
an ass
in my face
adorned
with
stretch marks —

smooth,
glistening scars
from her becoming
too much woman
too quickly.

so quickly
her pretty skin
couldn't keep up.

pretty ghosts in busy bars.

last night,
a pretty ghost
named becca
told me i feel much older
than twenty-seven
as we sat
in a red low-lit room
in a busy bar,
listening to a song
neither of us had ever heard
and before i could ask her
if she liked it,
she just vanished
into thin air
as if she were never even there.
she was either a ghost

or it was my schizophrenia.

she said:

"your
father
is
a
mess...

a
sweet
mess."

— momma,
july 31, 2019.

teal eyes.

her hands were pressed against
the face of a slightly awkward
baby-faced teenage boy
that was three years away
from looking like
marlon brando.

she was feeling his face
the way people do
when they can't see
what they so desperately
want to see,
the two of them
smiling smiles
that reached for miles
giving it away
that it wasn't the first time
she had felt his face
and it certainly wouldn't be
the last.

she worked her fingers
like a pianist
up his chin
and his lips
and his cheeks,
finally arriving

at his nose where she
playfully
squeezed it
in the way people squeeze things
they find too good to go
unsqueezed.

and they both laughed and once
they were finished laughing
she leaned into him
and he pressed his lips
above her right brow
and then sat his chin atop
her head like a crown.

they were silent now
as she looked my direction with a pair
of eyes
that almost looked teal
against the faded green seats
of the blue line.

she was pretty
but of a different kind
— a pretty
that doesn't set in until
you've had the chance to
look at her for a while
— a pretty that after a good
while of looking,

you realize to be the prettiest
in a room
(or a racing train car).

for a moment i felt myself grow sad,
wondering if perhaps she
had forgotten
just how pretty she was
or
if she had never seen
just how pretty she was.

but then i saw the way
the brando boy
held her in
the swaying car
and the way he looked at her
and the way he kissed her
and i felt less sad,
knowing she knew;
knowing he let her know,
over and over again.

years would pass,
quickly,
the way years do
and the boy would grow to look
like brando
and the girl with the teal eyes
would feel the walls of their homes

and the ears of their great big
german shepherd
that would lead her places
when he couldn't
and she would feel
the faces of their children
the same way she felt his
in that train car
and
the rest of the world
would watch on,
feeling as though
they themselves
were seeing
for the very first time.

perhaps.

the excitement of living
is thinking
so confidently
the world
is
one way
and
eventually finding
it is nothing
of the sort.

on missing without knowing.

do
you
ever
get
the
feeling
you're
missing
someone
you
have
not
yet
met?

this
is
how
i
felt
before
meeting
her.

we were damn close weren't we, love?

i hope she comes along
and turns my world upside down.

i hope we travel to far away places
and she'll be the only pretty face.

i hope we're rebellious
and we rant about how
we don't believe in the context of marriage
and then go ahead and do it anyway
because we can't stand the idea
of ever not being together.

i hope we're wild for a while.

i hope we spend our twenties
traveling
and fucking
and dancing
and partaking
in the occasional drug
and listening
to a vast array of live music.

i hope we eventually
semi-settle down
and find a house

near a city somewhere
but not in it.

i hope we say we don't want kids,
just dogs,
but one drunken night
we decide to take our chances
and it's the best chance we ever take.

i hope it'll be difficult
to find time to write
because i'll be so busy living the life
i said i'd never wanted
but wouldn't have any other way.

her.

let's set the scene.

i had caught a 6 a.m. flight to colorado
to meet a woman
that would eventually become
one of the great loves of my life
and i recall,
like it was the better part of yesterday,
feeling like a little boy
(not a twenty-five-year-old man)
as i sat,
cowering,
inside the slowly encroaching four walls
of a quaint coffee shop
called the black eye,
anxiously awaiting her arrival.

when she finally did show,
she was late,
something i found wildly ironic
considering i was the one
that had caught the flight
to attend the coffee date.
i'd later discover the reason
for her tardiness
was a digital debate
(via snapchat)
with her best friends regarding
her outfit-of-choice

for this fateful rendezvous
in denver's eclectic lo-hi district
(the neighborhood where the black eye
was and still is located to this day).

she eventually landed on something striking,
a black pinstripe jogger of sorts
that fit her like a glove
and a pair of big, clunky
doc martens
that i'd come to fall in love with
and the music they'd make
as they smacked against the pavement
like large pheasants too heavy to fly.

(isn't this the strangeness in love?
you find yourself batting away
jelly in the knees
over the most ordinary of moments —
like the way her boots sound
simply doing the very thing
they were created for,
walking,
or the strange aesthetic of the scar-tissue
she leaves behind on her nail beds
from her nervous,
incessant biting
or the way in which she brushes the bangs
from her pretty green eyes,
mid-conversation,

with those chewed-up nail beds.)

fuck,
did i fall in love with her.

and,
while all this is really very romantic,
the two of us met
(or reconnected, rather)
on instagram of all places,
which is extremely problematic
because the platform
has this remarkable way of
allowing us to fall head over *docs
for complete strangers,
and it allows us,
the strangers,
to dangerously craft these beautiful
(but wildly artificial)
facades and narratives of ourselves.

on instagram,
we're not unlike the recently renovated
picturesque
"historic" buildings,
smiling,
on bustling city blocks
housing coffee shops
and vintage thrift stores
and hot yoga studios

and urban outfitters
and lawyer's offices
— while our exteriors aren't necessarily
more pretty
nor less pretty
than our interiors,
they rarely,
if ever,
match.

however,
when i fell in love with the girl
i just hummed on about for the past —
i don't know, seven stanzas —
i'd like to think she was the exception to this rule,
that we were the exception to this rule,
that even now,
after everything that has happened,
we're still the exception to this rule.

the two of us grew up together
in southern indiana
and had a very short bout
where we dated for two,
maybe three weeks.
she moved away
and i moved away
and we lost touch
for the better part of a decade
but we followed each other on instagram

and sort of kept tabs on the other from afar.
what a strange phenomenon, huh?
how you can end with a person
at the age of fifteen
and then spend the next ten years,
watching their existence from afar.
it's at the same time beautiful
and toxic
like a zoo for your life's romances.

in the years that followed,
the two of us found ourselves
in and out of various relationships and,
at times,
dangerously close to one another —

well eventually,
we were in-between relationships,
at the same time,
and fighting a great deal of heartbreak,
at the same time,
because we both ended with humans
who meant a great deal to us.

(if there is any truth to human existence
it's that we are either falling in love
or falling out of love
and fighting desperately to navigate
both these heavens and hells.)

so,
one day,
i announced to my instagram "audience"

(i loathe that word
and recognize i am part of the problem)

that i would be writing a book
of poetry and prose,
page by page,
on the platform and that the book
would be called
"one minute, please?"
(you very well may have read it.)
with this announcement,
i shared my very first page.
she read this very first page
and she fell in love with it
and she wrote me
telling me
to keep writing.
she did this,
again
and again
and again.

to say this was a godsend
is an understatement.

i kept writing

and i'd be lying through my teeth
if i said i wasn't writing
every single page to her —
the sad pieces
and the happy pieces
and the pieces that found themselves
idling
between the two
like an awkward pre-teen
at a middle school dance
clinging to the room's shadows.

while i didn't write
"one minute, please?"
for her,
i wrote it to her.
and because of this,
she in many ways,
was the reason it was
breathed into existence.

i remember the feeling
i got on days she'd message me
and say:

this piece was particularly beautiful.

it was like cupid
had shot me three times
in the chest

and left me bleeding
in a pool of my own ecstasy.

for a good while,
my existence became about making the day
of this stranger who i hadn't laid eyes on
in-person for years,
this stranger who i was falling in love with
on instagram.

as these conversations developed,
one thing led to another
and eventually,
i wrote her and asked her
what she was doing
on a particular sunday afternoon.

to which she told me
she was doing nothing at all.
to which i responded that
i'd love to fly out
and take her to coffee.
to which she threw her phone on her bed
and covered her mouth
in a state of complete shock
and then little
by little
by little
by little
worked up the courage to say "yes".

to which i boarded a 6 a.m. flight
for a journey
that was intended to be a day or so
but ended up being seven.

after that,
the rest was a fucking fairytale
until it wasn't at all.
isn't this how most good things go?
they're as good as gold
until they're not anymore.
this is the tragedy in good things.

so i flew out,
and as i mentioned moments ago,
i found myself sitting,
nervously waiting,
for her to show —
nervousness that transformed
to nearly throwing up
the blue morphos
she adored
as i saw her step out of her suv
and out onto the pavement
and into the winter sun.
we spent the day
getting to know one another —
the real one anothers,
not the one anothers
we had portrayed on instagram.

she was a deeper thinker than she let on.
she was prettier than she was in her pictures.
her eyes popped more in person.
she was intelligent.
but, a different kind of intelligent —
like the kind of intelligent
an ambitious individual becomes
through real-world experience,
through taking one too many on the chin.
she was confident.
she was warm.
she was loving.
but,
at the same time terribly guarded.
that day
and much of our relationship
were spent dancing
in and out of the walls
she was constantly building —
at first i fought desperately
to pummel them down
but eventually accepted
they were as much a part of her
as the long brown hair
that fell down to her ass.

i fell in love with her
and when i boarded my flight home
i had this conviction

that i didn't want to spend
any more of my life
without her in it.

for the better part of a year,
we jumped at any chance we had
to see each other.
we boarded 6 a.m. flights
and high-tailed it across the country
to spend an afternoon
or two
in the same room,
in the same city,
in the same region.

she'd wake me up early
to catch the sunrises she adored.

she'd grab my chin
and make me look at the moon
she worshipped like religion.

she'd hold me tight to her chest
and neck
and face
when my head was a storm.

she'd laugh
when she caught me
taking myself too seriously

saying —
everyone thinks you're so serious
but i know you're just a goofball.

she'd snatch my hand into her's,
pulling me behind her,
showing me her favorite bars
and coffee shops
and eateries.

she'd turn on the shower
and ask me if i was joining —
when i was around
she hated taking showers
without me.

she'd whisper in my ear
late,
late
at night
that she wanted me
to one day father
her children
as she drifted off to sleep.

she'd sway,
the back of her body
pressed against mine,
as we listened to
post malone

and rainbow kitten surprise
and cigarettes after sex
and peach pit
and the list goes on
forever.

we were naive,
though.
and,
perhaps,
like everyone,
given a bad hand with the pandemic.
we didn't recognize at the time
that in order to weather the distance,
you must have a big beautiful black x
on the calendar
where you no longer have to —
a clear end.
otherwise,
one or both parties lose hope,
they lose touch
and the distance gives their mind
ample room to wander
and find resentment in the other person —
this cancer got to her first
and nearly overnight i noticed
she began to resent me
for not being in the same place as her
and for her own fears
and anxieties

i could never silence.
i'd constantly tell her
that i'd drink the bathwater
of her insecurities.
but,
this is the terrible trouble
with insecurities,
no amount of reassurance
will silence them.
one morning,
she phoned me
and she told me
she didn't have it in her anymore.
i tried to stop her
but realized,
that this time,
the wall she had built
without my knowing,
was too tall to climb
and too great to knock over
and too vast to dance around.
she had made up her mind.

and,
so now,
as i sit writing this piece in nashville,
1,156.7 miles away from her,
i'm experiencing the hell
of getting to unknow the person
i thought for a good while

i was going to live out my days with.
to aid in this unknowing,
i've found myself returning
to the very place
where we spent so much of our time,
early on,
back when we were just crushing hard
on one another from afar,
on instagram.
i'm attempting to fill the void
she left behind
with the very thing that made
the two of us possible —
and it's killing me.

so a few days ago,
i logged out of the app
for what i hope to be a ninety-day period
and decided to write this book.
i think a part of it is me trying,
desperately,
to give myself room to heal.
i think a part of it
is me trying to convince myself
that we still live in a world
where you can fall in love
by simply stumbling
into someone
at a wedding
or a coffee shop

or in the frozen section of a kroger.
i think
a part of it
is me trying to figure out
who cole is when january
isn't in the room.

and so far i keep coming up short.

docs.

i'll
tell
you
all
about
her —

she's
a
riot,

raising
hell,

fucking
my
sunday
to
pieces,

in
a
pair
of
road
worn
doc
martens

that
leave
her
ankles
bleeding.

earthsea.

like anything good,
she and i happened
slow at first,
then suddenly,
like the breaking of
a great damn
that
holds back
the sea.

she fucked around.

if
you're
not
careful,
love,
you're
gonna
fuck
around
and
become
my
human.

coming home.

finding your human
isn't unlike finding your home.
you have to see
and experience
and feel
and exist
in both pretty and unpretty places
that don't feel like home
and you must have the courage
to leave these places
and go to the next place
that very likely won't feel like home either.
and,
you do this,
again
and again
and again,
until one day you wake up
and there's an angel in your sheets
that you want to make breakfast for
and brew coffee for
and be the best version of yourself for,
and suddenly,
swiftly almost,
you decide to stay put for a while

— awhile or a lifetime.

& demons.

there
are angels
playing
in her hair.

do you see
the angels
playing
in her hair?

wrestling stilettos.

it's snowing.
her heel is caught
in an icy
grated outdoor staircase.
i told her not to wear them.
she wore them anyway
and now i'm squatting
and pulling
and wrestling it free.
it won't budge.
giggling,
she tells me to be careful
not to break it.
she's balancing on one leg,
her hands are on my shoulders.
finally it yanks free.
i carry her to the car
because there is
four inches of snow
on the ground
and i am wearing boots
and she's wearing the heels,
i told her not to wear,
the ones nearly
eaten by the stairs.
she's laughing.
flakes of snow are melting

on my naked head
we climb into the backseat
of a waiting taxi,
hot exhaust is billowing
from it's rear
like the chimneys
in vintage black and
white photographs
of cityscapes.
we buckle up,
she grabs my hand
like she's done it a
thousand times before.
i look at her
and then out the window
at the passing street lights.

kiss on her.

if there is a god,
he created me
to write pretty words,

and,
in-between the writing
of those pretty words,
kiss on her.

sex scene #7.

she's lying.
on her side.
her hair,
a messy knot.
held above her head,
by her own hand,
silencing gravity.
bumps appear
and then disappear
and then appear again,
down her spine,
her legs,
her arms.
her skin
becomes cold
and then callused
and then warm
and then smooth
as his lips brush
the lobes of her ears,
the nape of her neck,
the blades of her shoulders
and so on.
she's an instrument he's played
a thousand times.
he's yo-yo-ma,
grazing the cello.

he's hemingway,
strumming the royal.
he's van gogh,
going mad.
her back arches,
a comanche's bow.
it's beauty is lethal.
it kills him.
she kills him.
he grabs her waist,
slender.
removes a hand,
reaching for her neck.
the moon in the window
paints it as white
as a long winter.
he draws her near.
squeezing tighter.
she can't breath.
she doesn't want to.
he's full.
he's heavy.
he's steel,
sinking into her softness.
slowly at first,
then quickly.
an anchor tossed overboard.
as he sinks she sits deeper.
he releases her neck.
she gasps,

taking in a breath,
again full,
as if she's damned
to the bottom of the sea.
inside,
angels
and muses
and red devils playing violins
pull him,
yank him,
plead with him
to lose himself inside of her,
as if humanity depends on it.

miguel.

you're
too
damn
pretty
to
have
just
one
of
me

(but
please
tell
me
there
is
just
one
of
me).

theft.

you make me want to
steal that moon

you can't keep
your eyes
off of.

tiger.

she could be swapping,
in and out of pretty boys
like the fur jackets
the pretty girls wear
in belarus

but she tells me
tigers
don't need coats
to keep warm
in the wintertime.

quizzical brow.

when i watch her exist,
i'm not just watching her
as a man infatuated
but as a writer obsessed
with capturing every moment
of her existence.
a lifetime of
watching her
and existing with her
and loving her
would never be enough time.
i suppose i'm racing.

i'm racing
frantically.
scribbling
wildly,

sprinting to capture
the shooting star that is her
because it haunts me
to think
that one hundred years
from now
there will be a world
where she does not exist.

i'm writing to make her immortal.

bukowski.

i want
the entire fucking world
and you
and i will have
both,
before i am
through.

church camp.

she and i race
to litter the bedroom floor
with our clothes.
irony clings to the
corner of the room
like a rogue elephant.
we met a decade ago
in a church camp
both swearing off
sexual debauchery
like this.
a part of me blames god
as i go down on her.
he was over-zealous
in her creation.
her brain.
her beating heart.
her technicolor eyes.
her cascading hair.
her curves.
her pouty lips.
all of her is staggering.

he set all us kids up for failure.

breathe.

she
makes
love
to
me
like
it's
the
breath
that
is
keeping
me
alive.

swimming.

she's on her belly.

i'm lying on her.

my face,
nestled,
in the soft curve
of her back.

i ask her
if she thinks
that by saying things out loud
we jinx them
or manifest them?

she says nothing
for a while.
and then
she says
she hopes the latter.
i hope so too.
but,
i don't want to take
any chances.

so,
i keep mum.

and with this silence
the pretty thoughts
i have of a tomorrow with her,
swimming about my skull.

and,
looking back,
i probably should
have spoken up.

metrics.

i measure our love
in coffee mugs
and vinyl flips
and emptied wine bottles
and books that line our shelves
and your lipstick-stained cigarettes
that hunch over in the ashtray
like dead daisies.

we're floating.

this time
it's a bathtub.
it wears its claw feet
like high-heels.

she's lying on my chest
with her hair tied up into
something wonderfully messy.

her skin feels like wet velvet
against mine.

she's sipping
a heavy pour of
riesling.

i'm kissing her back,
my lips gathering up
droplets of her bathwater
like morning dew.

unfinished.

she
said
grab
my
face
and
kiss
me
mid-senten—

cream-colored.

i
can see your veins
keeping
you alive
like
indigo tracers,
oxidizing copper,
melting glaciers,
behind that pretty
white canvas
you call a back.

communion.

she's bowing
over the foot
of my bed
like she's
taking communion,
mouth open,
like she's
taking communion,
eyes closed
like she's
taking communion.
stark naked,
like she's
a dead catholic.
hair in my hands
like she's
giving me the reins.
pressed against me,
like she's
clinging to the edge of hell.

take me to church.

i have a cross around my neck.
i always wear it.
even when i dance with her
in the sheets.
i won't take it off.
i'll throw it behind my back
so god doesn't have to watch.

and,
while our bodies go
from cold to warm to hot,
the cross doesn't absorb
any of our heat,
it remains ice cold.
it's god
signaling his disapproval.

eventually,

the cross will slide
from the back
of my shoulder blades
and drop down,
falling atop
the curves of her breasts,
chilling her,
like an ice cube
on sunburnt skin.

kansas.

her back
is a terrain i've
trekked a thousand times.
it's bare,
it's white,
beautiful.
it's kansas
after a snowstorm,
a blank canvas,
unmolested,
gratified
only by
a thin brawl strap,
a few moles.

kimono.

every once
in a great while
the two of us
will find ourselves
in the same city
at the same time
and in the mornings
the sun will dance
through the windows
of whatever abode
we fell asleep in.
she and i will wake
still wearing nothing
from the night before.
i will wrap my arms and hands
around her to lie closer
and press my face
against the nape of her neck.
i'm darker than she is
but her skin is prettier
and together they contrast well,
like milk and honey.
on these precious mornings,
she wears me like
i was made for her;

she wears me like her kimono.

flowers picked.

it's a damn pretty
problem to have

—your girl
running out
of vases.

john richard.

we get into a grey nissan altima.
the driver introduces himself:

john richard.

he's from new york city
and he sounds like it.

he tells us he moved
to memphis for his girl.

he says he drives uber,
for two reasons:

to learn the city.

and, because his girl,
a nurse,
works three
twelve-hour shifts
each week and
the gig allows him
to have more quality time
with her.

he's got charisma.
we could listen to him

all day.

eventually,
i ask him what the dream is,
thinking nobody drives
uber to drive uber forever.

he says i'm looking at it.

he says he and his girl
have just enough money,
no more than they need.

he says tonight
when they get off work,
they're making
smoked salmon
and garlic potatoes.

he says that's all there is.

don't gasp.

i'm having coffee with her.
a little boy runs past,
falls,
his knees crash into the pavement.
i let out a bit of a gasp
or an ouch,
if you will.
like,
my fuck
that had to hurt.
she tells me not to do this.
she says it's not the pain
that makes little kids cry
when falling but the reaction of those
around them.
he starts to cry
as she is saying this.

i'm not sure
we ever grow out of this,
even as adults.
i don't think it's the pain of falling
that hurts us
but rather
the reaction to our falling
of those around us.

all of us are falling
constantly
and it takes courage
to fall
and it's extraordinarily difficult
to keep trying
and falling
when those around us are gasping
rather than applauding.

put me to sleep.

ambien.

it's grabbing your girl's hips,
pulling her into you,
feeling her warmth dance
over you
and your dick
and your thighs
and your stomach
and your chest
and your heart.

it's wrapping
your arms around her,
squeezing her
and her breasts
and her back
and her shoulders
and her soul.

it's burying your face
in the soft space
where her neck
meets the pillow.

pretty pictures.

my hands are
clutching my fujifilm.
it's pointing at her.
she's sitting on the countertop
across from me
in a pair of faded denim jeans
and a black cut off.
her hair is falling downward,
waterfalls of it on each side of her face.
behind her,
sun is creeping in
from a waffle-screened window,
casting dancing shadows
on the tile
and turning her hair
a rose gold.

she's camera shy —

i ask her to look at me.
she won't
i ask her to look at me.
she won't.
i ask her to look at me.
she does.

just for a moment.

then her eyes look away
and her eyelashes close
and she smiles gently
and i capture the moment.

unaware of how bad
pretty photographs hurt
1,000 miles away.

sonder.

like
rocks
in
my
pillow,
dreams
of
her
are
keeping
me
up
at
night.

idgaf.

i'm quite terrified
she will

find
a face prettier than mine.

i'm quite terrified
she will

kiss that pretty face
the way she does mine.

loathe.

i loathe instagram
specifically in regards to love.

i don't give a fuck
if my girl follows her ex
or if she likes pretty photographs
of pretty faced boys
or if pretty faced boys
like photographs of her.

i just don't want to see it.

and,
i feel like that's what instagram is.

it's seeing all the stuff
i don't give a fuck about
but it's making me give a fuck about it
because i'm seeing it.

close my eyes and hold on tight.

love is fiercely complicated,
terribly imperfect
and completely uncertain.
it will forever be this way
and i think to enjoy the ride
we must find beauty in its complication,
in its imperfection,
in its uncertainty.

instead
as romantics,
we find ourselves being swept away
by the single waves of love
most especially early on
when mere moments feel like light-years.
we read deep into the notes we send,
the silence between days,
the facial expression that seems off,
the passing comments.
we read into them
and we dissect them
and if we're not careful
we allow them to consume our minds
and our hearts
in such a frenzy
that we cost ourselves the ride.

"about today."

when
she's
far
away —

ask
her
why.

cityscape.

after dark,
we're on the rooftop
of my flat,
chicago
on the horizon.
it's glaring at us.
she is glaring at me.
i'm smoking a cigarette
doing my best james dean.
i tell her she looks nice.
she's mad at me
because i make her feel things
and her feeling things
makes her feel out of control.
i hand her my cigarette,
something to hold on to,
anything,
to make her world
stop spinning.
i motion for it
back,
my world
starts spinning,
too.

the latter, i hope.

love,
i
see
this
going
one
of
two
ways:

us
running
from

or

to.

gone missing.

missing someone is:

jumping on a big jet plane
with a sticky face
from her glossy kisses.

warring with a thudding in your skull,
a side-effect of three bottles of red wine
with her at 2 a.m.

popping advil at altitude
to stop the thudding,

slipping on shades
to stop the thudding,

in between the thudding
fighting like hell
to black the motion pictures
of her naked body,
intertwined
in a labyrinth of
white linens.

grabbing for your denim jacket,
in need of a blanket,
smelling,

wondering how the fuck
her scent followed you
31,000 feet into the air,

looking down out the cabin window
and not seeing snow.

lifeline.

i'm wildly in love
with the day

jet planes

and late night
telephone rings

are no longer

the lifelines

holding us
together.

lonesome rose.

doing any sort of distance
successfully
is about knowing
that there will be moments
(many many moments)
you feel farthest away
from the person you
are closest too;
and it's about deciding
whether or not
that kind of fucked up,
emotionally draining,
mentally exhausting
existence
is worth it.

fiction.

it's a tennessee fall evening.
cool.
the loveliest kind of cool.
she and i are leaning up
against a brick wall,
sitting.
she's a sad-eyed model
with a pretty voice.
when she speaks
she sounds like winehouse.
i could listen to her forever.

between pulls from her cigarette
she tells me about her human.

she says he's just a stone's throw away.

you throw a stone on a big jet plane
and if it goes fast enough,
eventually,
it will find him.

i tell her that's a lovely way to put it
(but terribly dramatic)
and she agrees
and she laughs
and she stops laughing

because she's hurting
and she keeps telling me
about this human of hers
and i listen because i like her voice
and because it makes me miss hers,
less.

trouble.

most of life's trouble
stems from the distance
between
two points.
the distance between
you
and your life's work.
the distance between
you
and the person
you want to be.
the distance between
you
and that girl
across the fucking world.

most of life's trouble stems
from the grey space between
what we have
and what we want
and the frenetic
emotionally charged anxiety
that exists
around the possibility
of us not ever getting it.

cab.

i call her a cab

(i'm referring to it as a cab
because there is absolutely nothing
romantic about an uber)

and drop her bags in the trunk.

she kisses me with
her glossy lips
leaving some of its thick glow
behind on my own.

and,
she rushes away
to the airport,
and i'm standing
in the chicago cold
thinking about the strangeness
of lip gloss.

it's lovely to have on your lips
when you know
you can wake up next to the pretty face
that painted it there.

less so when you can't.

i think all of this,
more or less,
as i watch
the red taxi fade into nothing,
darting farther
and farther
up the street.

i think about how much,
in this moment,
her
lip gloss
is the last thing in the world
i want to taste.

getaway.

honey,
i can't love you —

not with your car still running
in the driveway.

2 a.m.

you can leave
anytime you'd like,
just be sure to pack up
your things
before you go.

i don't want to discover
your hair-ties
making love to my toes
as i wake
in the middle of the night

to take a piss.

how pretty things end.

most pretty things end
not in the way you'd think.

one person goes quiet
then the other person goes quiet.

and then both persons wait for the other
to speak up,
to say something,
anything,
to break the silence.

but,
the stories
they're telling themselves
are louder than the silence
so they listen to those stories instead
and,
eventually,
they decide they're better off
just starting a new conversation
with someone else.

after her.

dead on impact.

we didn't make it.
we couldn't go the distance.
but my god did we fight.
you should have seen
the way we fought.
against gravity.
against inevitability.
against the end.

we fought.

like the other's soul
depended on it.

we fought.

like the other was
clinging to the edge of hell.

we fought.

like the devil's tongue was
licking our heels.

you nearly killed me.

you wake up one morning
finding the morning
is different than the morning before
not in the way the sun paints the window pane
nor in the rat-tat-tat the house flies make
like tiny djs
as they attempt the impossible:

breaking through the sun-painted window pane
to raise hell in tennessee.

the morning is different in the way
your bed takes on the shape of her
like an angel fell asleep
in the midst of a snowstorm
leaving nothing visible to the rest
of us mortals save for
locks of hair,
and a rose-colored cheekbone
accented by long lashes
van gogh would've given
his last remaining ear to sling paint with.

and, since you're not
hannibal lecter you don't watch
her sleep —

i once woke up to a pretty bitch
watching me sleep and it was
the last time we slept together

— but you more or less exist there with her,
feeling that living breathing mound of snow
rise and fall, rise and fall, rise and fall
and you pray to god and the universe
that you have the goddamn sense
to coax her into lying there,
right by your side,
for the rest of your life.

you won't, of course.
you'll lose her.

one morning,
perhaps on the fourth of july,
she'll phone you
and you'll answer
and she'll say goodbye
and you'll let her go
and that'll be the end of it.

for a good while,
you'll tell yourself
it's going to be okay
because that handsome sonofabitch,
steinbeck,
once wrote in a letter

to his heartbroken son that...

"nothing good gets away."

but then your imagination
drowns out that line
like coyotes do the quiet of night.
your imagination does
what imaginations do
and it starts creating the next man
she'll fall in love with.

my imagination created
an incredibly good-looking man
with more hair atop his head,
with a bigger dick,
with nicer looking tattoos (and more of them),
with a stronger more defined jaw
she just cut her fingers on.

he's now sucking them.

it's here where you start recovering,
not entirely,
never entirely,
but somewhat,
enough to get by.
you get loaded off whiskey
and you sit with this man
alone in a room,

and you riff with him
and you laugh with him
and you try like hell to like him
and then, eventually, once you're ready
(never before you're ready)
you get the fuck up from your seat,
you walk across the room,
you shake the man's hand
and you exit stage left.

it's here when you quit instagram.

not because of her
but because you do some digging
and realize all the pretty bitches
whispering in your ear
in that virtual fucking world
sent the plane into a spiral.

you realize that even though
you aren't fucking the gal
that looks like a porn star
living somewhere in nebraska
nor the gal in berlin
you're romanticizing the possibility
of fucking them
and that makes it incredibly difficult
to carry on a relationship
with the living breathing human being
lying next to you now as you're reading this.

you quit.
and you find that you can look yourself
in the mirror again.
you don't have her back
but you have the next best thing
— yourself.

so you take yourself
and you dress in blue
and you show up
to your best friend's wedding
and you sit your ass down
in the church pew
and pray to god
the three day bender
you've been on
doesn't burn the mahogany black
and you find yourself sweating
like a whore in church
(you are a whore in church)
as you watch your best friend sob
as he watches his best friend
walk down the aisle.

and you start crying too
because you love him
almost as much as you love yourself
and you're wildly proud of him
because he had the sense

not to let the snow melt.

you get in your car,
you drive home to tennessee.
he and his gal run off to colorado
for their honeymoon.
you scratch your head
at the irony of it all.
on the way home you listen to
lana del ray
and while you don't know
a fucking thing
about long beach
you find yourself missing
the lower highlands
and the black eye
and el five
and her.

and you say oh well
and decide it might be time
to find yourself a venice bitch
which proves to be difficult
because the venice bitches
read your writing
and know all your lines
and all your insecurities
and all your fears
and the fact that you're a serial killer
that mows down pretty girl's hearts

for pretty words.
and you show up
to these first dates,
completely naked,
from head to toe,
as they're fully clothed
and you wonder
what they want to talk about first...
what the fuck happened in colorado
or what the fuck happened in that bathroom
when you were five years old.

instead, the two of you talk about the weather
(thank mother nature for the weather).
and hope that it doesn't prove to be daily.
and when the clock strikes twelve
and everyone's asleep you get drunk
and you write a book called *after her*;
because it's damn lonely without her
and you must give yourself something to read.

forever;

love

is

promising
one
another
the
world

until

someone
changes
their
mind.

literary murder.

we can kill love
rather quickly.

it begins with
the stories
we tell ourselves,

continues with
us believing them
and ends with
us eventually
deciding it's time
to close the book.

distance v. dailyness.

there is distance
and there is dailyness
and i'm not sure love can exist
fully
in either extreme.
there needs to be
a middle ground
between the two.

distance gives us room
to long
and to crave
and to miss.
but,
too much distance
forces us to build walls
to protect our hearts
from the uncertainty
of not seeing someone.

dailyness gives us time
to get comfortable,
to feel warm,
to settle in.
but,
too much dailyness
causes us

to take a person for granted —

there is a middle ground.
i am certain of it.

i just don't know where it is.

more on dailyness.

i will be around
until you start looking at me
like that ugly blue vase
or that wispy light fixture
or that painting on the wall.
i will be around
until you start looking at me like
something to be expected,
like something daily,
like something you've grown so used to
(and perhaps tired of),
like something that just simply
occupies your world.
when you start looking at me
like i'm a wallflower
i'll disappear from your life
and you won't notice a thing
and i'll move far away
and exist in front of another set
of pretty eyes
that light up when they see me.
i'll exist there
until her eyes
begin to pass over me,
too.

silent night.

you
don't
fall
out
of
love,

you
just
run
out
of
things
to
talk
about.

linger.

there is this haunt
called linger.
once upon a time
it was a mortuary,
which is just a fancy word
for a morgue.
but,
today it exists as a bar of sorts.
the moscow mules there are good
and they are cold
and if you're drinking alone,
you're never truly drinking alone.

linger means to stay in a place
longer than necessary
because of a reluctance to leave.
i think there are a few somethings
lingering there
for some reason or another
and i'd buy them a drink
if i could.
but,
i can't.

and,
it's all very odd,
because i think humans

and ghosts
have more in common than we realize.
it's this odd propensity to linger...

to stay in a place longer than necessary

because of a reluctance to leave.

stan.

the only love for me
is the overzealous,
gripping,
addictive,
all-consuming,
fuck me up
in the best kind of ways,
love.

and,
i think that's why
i don't last long
in love.

when it goes from
stan to stale
i make my french exit
through the backdoor
carrying memories
of the pretty things
she said to me,
back when she thought
i hung the moon.

drive.

i've taken a backseat in her world
for a while now,
and none of it is her fault.

the world throws all sorts
of unexpected things at us,
and it forces us to make choices.

tough choices.

i just seem to never be on the
right side of these choices.

and i don't hate her,
i hate the situation,
but i don't hate her.

regardless,
sooner
or later,
i've got to get the fuck out,
i'm a caged jaguar back here,
i'm a caged jaguar back here,
i'm a caged jaguar back here.

actually,
pull over,

up here,
at this gas station,
i'll walk the rest of the way,
i'll walk until
i find a vintage range rover
with green patinated paint
i'll jump in,
light the ignition.
i'll drive.
i'll be the king again.

fireworks.

she
phones
me
at
10:37 a.m.
on
the
4th
of
july,

at
10:51 a.m.
she
says
goodbye

and,
just
like
that
my
daughter
no
longer
has
her
eyes.

01/05/1994.

she
feels
like
january
burning
to
the
ground.

to those heartbroken.

heartbreak manifests in unusual ways.
you feel it everywhere but your heart.
you feel it in the back of your throat,
in the pit of your stomach,
and in your skull at night
when your head hits the pillow
and your mind is racing to
the person
that once was your person
once upon a time.
i'm not sure where in our bodies
our souls exist,
but they scream to us
in these places...

in our throats
and stomachs
and skulls.

and,
while i can't make
the heartbreak go away
i can tell you something
that has always helped me —

make good art.

it burns like the clap.

i know.
it burns like the clap.

her pretty face,
everywhere.

especially,
on the backs of the eyelids
she used to kiss.

look at you,
prying them apart,
putting off the moment
you must dream of her.

killing me softly.

heartbreak feels like an endless falling.
it feels like you're falling,
forever and then some —
waiting,
pleading,
hoping
you'll come crashing into the pavement.
(but the pavement never comes).
it feels like
falling
and not knowing
when you're going to stop falling.

late, late.

there are
dark nasty corners
in your mind
littered with cobwebs
and black widows
and red devils playing violins

and her

— stay far away from these places

late, late
at night.

clocked.

i
can't
seem
to
find
the
time
to
make
myself
feel
better
again.

last night.

a dream.
light clings to my room's corner
like a house cat
who has suffered a bad fright.
its brilliance
echoes
from a single flame
burning deep in the barrel of a candle
that's running out of fuel.
it licks the air
in short curtailed strokes,
a tiny van gogh
sending dancing shadows
up the walls
and the ceilings.
she's lying on top of me.
she looks like margot robbie.
she is margot robbie.
her blue eyes,
colorless,
in the night.
save for the moments
when the tiny painter
looks our way.
beneath her,
wet.
a wetness

that feels like
a tennessee summer:
hot,
inescapable,
drowning.
she kisses me
like she's
tapping a
maple tree
for sweetness.
she falls down
my lips
and my neck
and my chest
and my stomach
venturing to the
place where
it runs most
true.
she gives me
head
like she
doesn't know
how to say
i love you.

left for dead.

fuck me
like a scorpio

(just leave me breathing).

next.

the
bitch
in
all
of
this
is
she
is
looking
at
me
the
way
you
used

to.

margot robbie.

i'm stealing moments
with this nurse
who looks like
margot robbie.

she works the night shift,
delivering babies.

sometimes
i want her to deliver mine.
sometimes
i want her to have mine.

we haven't
slept together.
i can't believe
we haven't
slept together.

i keep lying to myself:

i'm not catching feels
i'm not catching feels
i'm not catching feels

yesterday,

i asked her
how she takes her coffee.

iced
and with almond milk.

ambulance.

i'm a paramedic,

a self-educated
paramedic,

patching up holes
in my chest
from the claws
of the woman
who came before the woman
who came before you.

loving me,

it might be a mess,

warring with all this
needle and thread

like running,
headlong
into spider web
on a no moon
night.

literature.

love,
you can't have
my heart.
i don't even have
my heart.
it's missing,
everywhere.
it's running
barefoot
on green grasses
in southern indiana.
it's drunk
on poetry
along the coast of
pensacola.
it's wandering,
sleepily,
the streets
of minsk.
it's a thousand miles
in the air,
hovering,
like a cloud,
watching over colorado.
but
you can have
something,

i swear to god
i do have something left
in here
to give.

r/un.

the
saddest
story
in
the
world
is
someone
falling
in
love
with
someone
falling
out.

bad dream.

bad dream.
my teeth are falling
out of my mouth
onto the bathroom
floor
like dead doves.
bad dream.
the hardwood floor
in my home is
coming undone
like bad stitches,
gaps are forming
gaps are widening
gaps are giving way
to more gaps,
in-between the gaps
i see hell.
bad dream.
we're sitting
next to one another
on a big jet plane,
you're holding my hand.
out the window
a dead dove that is my teeth
gets sucked into the engine.
you look at me,
eyes wide and eyes green,

we're going down.
i wake up
a sweaty mess
with an erection
so hard it hurts.
i've got to take
a piss.
but have to figure
something out
or risk pissing
on my chin.
i pry it down
and lean
my forehead
and my off-hand
against the
wall at a
forty-five degree
angle.
the piss hits
the toilet water
like a laser pistol.
i feel better.
bladder, empty.
cock, half-mast.
i look in the mirror.
i smile.
my teeth look
unsteady, foreign,
like they belong

in someone
else's mouth.
i touch one
and the rest
fall out like
dead doves.
bad dream.
i wake up again.
this time for real.
it's 1 a.m.
i need a drink.
i call a taxi.
the taxi shows.
it's piloted by
a hispanic gent
named diego.
diego is old.
diego is plump.
diego is a good man.
diego starts talking
about his wife.
he says he met her
in a laundromat
in new york city.
he says she said hello,
first.
he says she just waved
and smiled
and couldn't stop
smiling.

there is a very
long pause
the type of pause
that feels like
you have to pull
out the dvd
and cover it
in toothpaste.
diego finally says,
i miss her.
in a strange way,
i miss her too.
i miss her for diego.
he says
she died a little while back.
he says he lost everything
in his home because he
couldn't physically go back.
later,
at the bar
dead of night.
the night is so
dead it's becoming
a phoenix,
sprouting wings
and turning
into a new day,
almost morning.
i order a
miami vice

from the bartender.
he says the machine
is down.
i say a mule,
kentucky.
over my kentucky
mule i decide
it's really time
i start believing
in the man i've got
hanging around my neck.
so i can believe in heaven,
so i can believe diego
and his wife will
see each other again.
that night i put
my cellphone underneath
my bed
so in the morning i have
to get down on my hands
and knees to grab it
and it will remind me
to pray.
in the morning.
i get down on my hands
and knees and i don't know
what to say.
i say...
"god,
it's been so long since

we've last talked
and i don't know what
to say.
there is a long pause."
i say...
"god,
please,
tell me what to say.
there is a long pause."
i say...
"fuck it."
i lean up
and hit my head
on the bed frame.
later that night
a gal who looks
like lana del rey
gives me head
to lana del ray
atop that bed sitting atop that
bed frame.
she sucks my dick like a gemini
like she's got two faces,
two mouths.
heaven and hell.
i come.
she swishes me around her mouth
like listerine.
then spits me out
over the balcony,

eight floors up,
and what
could have been
my kids
had they been
in the right place
at the right time
hit the
pavement
like dead doves.
she jumps down after them.
bad dream.
i wake up,
again.
it's just a dream.
my cellphone rings.
it's underneath the bed.
dead in the middle
like the dead doves
like those green eyes
like diego's heart.
i get down on my hands
and on my knees
and i crawl through
the barbed wire
that is that
fucking bed frame
only to see there's no number
on the phone.
it just says:

unknown.
i don't pick up.
scared to death

it's god.

time machines.

there are
so many
things
i'd like
to say
to you,
but
they're about
forever ago,
and
i try
desperately
not
to play in
time-machines.

blackberry kisses.

i'm a kid.
my mom and dad pack me into a van
with my two brothers.
we race to quebec.
my mother's aunt lives there.
her name is martha.
when we arrive she gives me a basket.
she points to a bush
up the road.
she tells me to pick blackberries
so she can make me a blackberry pie.
i pick them and pick them
until there aren't any left to pick.
they stain my fingers
this beautiful black hue.
i eat them, too.
i pick the bush clean
and an hour later
there is a blackberry pie
and ten minutes after that,
there is no blackberry pie.
my brothers and i ate all of it.
years later,
i meet this girl
and i steal kisses from her
like the blackberries
from that bushel and eventually,

they all run out,
as kisses and blackberries
have a way of doing.
and,
it's terribly sad.
terribly sad.
but,
it's lovely too.
i can still taste them,
like those blackberries
i ate as a kid
and i still have
her beautiful hue on me,
too.
they're memories now
and from time to time
they fuck me to pieces,
but you should taste how
sweet they are
and you should see
how the hue of her glows
behind closed eyelids,
late at night
when i'm floating off a bottle of wine
wondering if maybe just maybe,
there were more blackberries
left to be had.

starman.

love,
don't go dancing
in time-machines.
you will want to,
from time to time.
you will want to reach out
and grab for the hand you let go of
so long ago,
to see if you can't
drop the needle
on the vinyl
where the music last stopped.
but nothing good comes
from time-traveling
because nothing good gets away.

nothing good gets away.

how to get rid of ghosts.

eventually,
you have to do away with her clothes.
you throw on a good vinyl.
something you fell in love with
after her.
then you thumb through her closet,
pulling out pieces of her
and letting them pile
in a small heap
at your feet.
i'd do your damndest to breathe
out of your mouth
and not your nose.
i imagine her scent still lingers there,
intertwined deep in the fabrics.
once they're lying lifeless on the closet floor,
parachute open a trash bag
and place them in,
one by one.
grab a cigarette,
head to the thrift store,
see if you can get enough for a moscow mule.
the merchant will be your hitman.
he's not emotionally involved.
take the money.
head to a good pub,
one with an elbow worn bartop,

countless scars from other broken men like you
who've drunk entire afternoons away.
order a mule,
on her.
then,
smoke a cigarette
without her.
walk home and her ghost should be gone.

but, i'm trying.

the devil
in all of this,
love,
is that
i don't know how
to move on
with my own life,

while
still holding onto
the possibility
of a life with
you.

on choosing.

choosing
to love someone
is
choosing
to let them
break your heart.

it's not a question
of if.
but,
rather a question
of when.

you love someone
long enough
and hard enough,
eventually,
they'll do something human
and you'll be left
nursing
the heart
you gave them

to be human with.

all for everything.

when we love someone
we should put every
ounce of ourselves
into helping them grow
into the person they were
put on this earth to be,

even if that person
isn't the person we
originally fell in love with.

even if that person
isn't the person that
originally fell in love with us.

casablanca.

i want her to find that
timeless
colorful,
radiant
sort of love
we see in those
old black and white pictures
that seem to go on
forever
and ever
and ever.

do(n't).

if i ever have a son of my own,
i will tell him to be
extraordinarily careful,
falling for pretty girls
in faraway places.

i will tell him,
as i speed him to the airport,
making certain he doesn't miss his flight.

to whomever loves her next.

she takes oat milk in her lattes.
she adores sunsets
(but sunrises more).
she follows the zodiac
like it's religion
and she won't hear
an ounce of skepticism about it.
she loves her friends
like kanye loves kanye
and can be just as irrational.
she apologizes.
but,
it takes her a moment.
give her that moment.
the battle scars on her ankles
are from her breaking in her
doc martens.
it's an obsession.
she'll add to her collection once a year.
remind her to double up on socks.
when she gets out of sorts,
take her outside to look at the moon.
or,
hand her a glass of red wine.
or,
throw on some post malone.
or,

a flick with mcconaughey in it.
or,
have her do something creative
(she's dying when she's not creating).
and,
for the love of god...
please don't be allergic to cats.
like,
the unlucky fellow who came before you.
she's lightyears better with one
roaming around her space,
like a lioness in miniature.
she is a lioness in miniature.

tiger tail.

i remember
one trip out to colorado
to see her,
she handed me
a gold-plated towel hook
that took on the shape of a tiger,
curiously glancing
over its right shoulder,
showing the world
its striped back,
its tail,
hanging,
making a gentle hook.

i remember
her handing it to me,
smiling,
saying nothing,
nothing at all,
just pressing her lips
against mine,
unknowing
it was so much more than nothing
to me;
unknowing
that it was everything to me.

i remember
having to leave her,
and replacing the warmth of her hand
with that gold-plated tiger-in-miniature,
its tail snaking around the back of my hand
like a gentle embrace,
as i road in the taxi to the airport
where i'd board a plane to take me home.

i remember,
later on,
hanging it up.

i remember
people coughing up guillotines.
i remember
no longer boarding those flights
and i remember
feeling like a drowning man
with his legs tethered
to the bottom of the cumberland,
reaching out my hands
in breathless desperation
for my heart
and my soul
and for her,
frozen in place,
mountainside,
1,156.7 miles away.

i remember,
for a long time,
barely hanging on.

i remember
one day
breathing again.
although,
i can't remember when.
i remember
waking up
and feeling as though
it was all a distant dream;
that it all had happened
to someone else,
someplace else.
i remember
having coffee one morning,
thinking of her,
and being relieved to find
the thought didn't kill me anymore,
that it just left me feeling
thankful
having known whatever it was
we had.

and,
one day,
some day,
i will remember

these days,
these days
i'm living in now,
where she only breaks my heart
but once a day
and only for a moment's time;
a moment
i cannot help but welcome
with open arms —

i will remember
every night,
at 9 p.m.,
washing away the day
with soap and water,
stepping out of the shower,
wicking away the droplets
that cling to me
like morning dew.

i will remember
closing my eyes
as i hang my towel
on a tiger's tail
that clings
to the walls of my home

like a memory terrified to let go.

the end.

i'm so sorry,
love.

but,

i have to stop
writing

about us,

now.

January Black.

Most author bios are written in the third person which makes absolutely no fucking sense. If I saw someone talking about themselves in the third person at a dinner party (*not that I attend many dinner parties*), I'd think them to be an asshat.

Anyway, my name is January Black. I'm the alter ego of a gent named Cole Schafer. I wrote this book. I've written other books. I plan to write a great deal more before I bite the dust.

If you want to learn more about myself, just re-read this book or pick-up a copy of *One Minute, Please?* If you'd like to learn more about Cole Schafer (*though, I'm afraid, he isn't very interesting*), I'd take a peek at his Instagram (*@cole_schafer*) where he shares pretty pictures (*and words*).

Or, I would peruse Cole's creative writing shop (*www.honeycopy.com*) where he writes advertising for many of the brands you buy. I, unfortunately, don't have any affiliation with Honey Copy. In fact, Cole doesn't let me anywhere near the shop, concerned I might try and fuck one of his clients.

All that to say, thank you for reading. It made my little scribbler's hearts burst with joy. I'd lick you but this is a book and you can't lick people through books. At least not right now. Perhaps in 2050. My God, will *Fifty Shades of Grey* be a wildly different book in 2050

– *January.*